WILLIAMSBURG

A Picture Book to Remember Her by

CRESCENT BOOKS
LAKE COUNTY NEW YORK

CLB 1992
© 1987 Colour Library Books Ltd., Guildford, Surrey, England.
Printed and bound in Barcelona, Spain by Cronion, S.A.
All rights reserved.
1987 edition published by Crescent Books, distributed by Crown Publishers, Inc.
ISBN 0 517 64787 7
h g f e d c b a

For all its importance to the history of America, Williamsburg's heyday lasted less than sixty years. When Thomas Jefferson was elected governor in 1779, British troops had already passed through Williamsburg and were threatening to come back. Jefferson proposed that the capital be moved to Richmond and when his advice was taken a year later, Williamsburg became a sleepy little college town again.

Even its history was largely forgotten by 1903 when the Rev. Dr. W.A.R. Goodwin accepted the call to become rector of Bruton Parish Church. A town native, he was dismayed by the decay that had set in even in his lifetime. He was passionate about changing it for the better, and within four years he had raised enough money to restore his church to its original splendor in time for the 300th anniversary of the Episcopal Church in America. But nobody thought the whole town would ever be restored.

Dr. Goodwin moved on to Rochester, New York in 1909 and returned in 1923 to join the faculty of William and Mary. He came back with his enthusiasm intact and fortunately was able to pass some of it along to the philanthropist John D. Rockefeller, Jr. Almost no one in town didn't agree that the combination of Dr. Goodwin's passion and Mr. Rockefeller's money was the best thing that happened to Williamsburg since Governor Nicholson gave up the idea of having its streets laid out in the form of a William and Mary monogram.

On February 24, 1934, less than six years and $12 million after the restoration began, the Virginia Assembly crowded itself into the Capitol at Williamsburg for the first time in more than 150 years and officially welcomed the past back to Virginia.

The building isn't the original, but it would fool any of the original settlers. The old capitol, like so many of the Williamsburg buildings, had long since disappeared. But they have been rebuilt using original plans and, whenever possible, materials from the same sources.

The Williamsburg restoration is one of the most ambitious architectural projects of the 20th century. Millions have walked its streets and taken away ideas that have changed the face of other towns all over America. It created a national interest in "recycling" rather than destroying old buildings. And all the current interest in "early American" architecture and decoration can be traced directly to this recreation of Colonial Williamsburg. The Keeper of the National Register of Historic Places had said that Williamsburg is the "formulator of popular 20th century taste" in America.

What could be more appropriate? In its relatively short life as Virginia's capital, Williamsburg was almost the formulator of America itself.

Facing page: the Peyton Randolph House, once home to of one of the most prominent families in Colonial Virginia.

When Governor Nicholson laid out the plans for the new capital of the colony of Virginia he included in them a central avenue one mile long and 99 feet wide. Along Duke of Gloucester Street (overleaf), as it was called, stand Margaret Hunter's millinery shop (right), John Blair's House (far right), the Sign of the Rhinoceros Apothecary Shop (above), the Peyton Randolph House (top right) and Merchants Square (top).

Facing page top left and overleaf right: the reconstructed form of the Raleigh Tavern, an important building in the history of Williamsburg, and (overleaf left) the Pasteur-Galt Apothecary Shop. Carter's Grove (above, left and above left), with its magnificent woodwork by English craftsman Richard Baylis, has been called "the most beautiful house in America." Below: the ballroom and (facing page bottom) the kitchen of the Governor's Palace.

Traditional crafts are kept alive in Williamsburg by costumed staff who lend an authenticity to the practices of basket weaving (above and facing page) and jewelry making (left). Craftsmen also work in the Magazine (bottom), where ammunition was held during the French and Indian War. Period tools are used in the making of the colonial reproductions which may be bought in the Historic Area's stores. Overleaf: Archibald Blair House.

The wheelwright's workshop (bottom) was a busy place, servicing the carts (left) and carriages that travelled the Colonial roadways. Facing page: the Governor's Palace and (below) Robertson's Windmill.

Archaeological excavations were invaluable in the re-creation of Prentis House (facing page top). Facing page bottom: Anthony Hay's Cabinetmaking Shop. Left: Levingston Kitchen, (below) Deane Forge and Harness-making Shop and (above) Nicolson's Shop.

DEANE
SHOP
AND
FORGE

Colorful military displays (below, bottom, right and overleaf) are staged frequently in Colonial Williamsburg. Facing page: a musketeer holding his musket and the paper cartridge of gunpowder with which he will charge it, and (bottom right) a cannon in Market Square.

The Margaret Hunter Shop (top) is a veritable treasure trove of Colonial ladies' finery: a 1774 advertisement offers "Jet necklaces and ear-rings, black love ribands, Sleeve Knots, Stuff Shoes for Ladies, Women's and children's riding habits, dressed and undressed Babies, toys, scotch snuff, and Busts of the late Lord Botetourt". Right: the cobbler and (above, facing page and overleaf) costumed staff.

Above and top: traditional baking with authentic ingredients is carried out in restored kitchens on old-fashioned ranges. Weaving (left) and candle making (facing page) may also be watched on a tour of the town's many craft workshops.

Left: a carriage in Market Square and (bottom) Norton-Cole House, one of the few 19th-century structures that has been preserved in Williamsburg. Below: George Wythe House, home to one of the most influential Americans of his time. The Pasteur-Galt Apothecary Shop (facing page) is faced with simulated stone, a fashion adopted in the 18th century. Overleaf: (left) the General Court inside the Capitol and (right) the Margaret Hunter Shop.

Facing page: (top) Bryan House and (bottom) Merchants Square, one of America's first planned shopping centers. Below right: Prentis Store, Williamsburg's best example of an original Colonial store, and (above) the Raleigh Tavern.

The importance of wood in Colonial times was great – housing, vehicles, tools and furniture were all chiefly constructed from timber – and this is reflected in the crafts carried out in Williamsburg today. This page: carpenters using traditional methods. Facing page: a cobbler and (overleaf) a timber yard.

Chowning's Tavern (bottom) catered to a less dignified class of patron than some of its neighbors in colonial times, but welcomes all today to sample its specialties of Brunswick stew, oysters and "Chowning's good bread." Left: the sign of Edinburgh Castle outside Burdett's Ordinary. Facing page: the tiny cobbler's in Duke of Gloucester Street.

Previous pages: the backs and distinctive oval-plan garden of the reconstructed Orlando Jones House and Office. Facing page: (top) traditional fare and utensils on display in the kitchen of the Governor's Palace, and (bottom) the interior of Bruton Parish Church. Taking its name from a town in Somerset, England, this church was the most important public building in Middle Plantation before William and Mary College was built. Above: Robertson's Windmill, (right) the Davidson Shop, (above right) the tiny Boot and Shoemakers and larger Greenhow-Repiton House and (top right) the Prentis Store.

Facing page: Bruton Parish Church. It was a rector of Bruton Parish, the Reverend W. A. Goodwin, who first conceived a plan to restore Williamsburg and engaged the enthusiastic help of John D. Rockefeller, Jr. in this project. Right: the Courthouse of 1770 on Market Square (bottom). Below: a carriage awaits in Duke of Gloucester Street. Overleaf: Timson House.

Most gentlemen wore wigs in the eighteenth century, made to measure by the wigmaker whose craft is still practiced in the King's Arms Barber Shop (previous pages left). Previous pages right: (top) Coke-Garrett House, (bottom left) the Prentis Store and (bottom right) Wetherburn's Tavern. These pages: parades, celebrations and salutes play an important role in Williamsburg's colorful tribute to its past. Left: musketeers fire a "Volley of Joy" on July 4. Overleaf: the octagonal Magazine which served as the arsenal for the entire Virginia colony. Erected in 1715, the original building – a "good substantial house of brick" – still stands today.

Facing page: a house on Market Square. The Golden Ball (right) was the workplace of James Craig, esteemed jeweler and silversmith, whose skills are copied by the craftsmen here today. Top: George Whythe House, a solid brick mansion standing on the west side of Palace Green and (above) the rebuilt Blue Bell.

The extent of the influence of the Carter family in Williamsburg is apparent in the fine homes that bear their name. Carter's Grove (bottom left and bottom right) was owned by five generations of the family, and Robert Carter lived in a house (facing page) on Palace Street for 12 years. Left: the luxurious Council Chamber in the Capitol (below), where the colony's appointive members met and served at the behest of the Crown. Below left: a carriage in Market Square.

Previous pages: a fife and drum band provides the music in a parade outside Archibald Blair House. Facing page: the sign of the Raleigh Tavern, the most famous of Williamsburg's taverns, dedicated to the man who played such a large part in sending colonists to the New World. Left and below: the State Garrison Regiment and Williamsburg Militia celebrate July 4 on Market Square. Above: a mechanism used for lifting a cannon barrel onto its carriage. Overleaf: Orlando Jones House.